T0158994

TRAGEDY
to
TRIUMPH
The Path to Police Magic

Glenn Hester

Foreword by
James Munton

TRAGEDY TO TRIUMPH
THE PATH TO POLICE MAGIC

iUniverse books may be ordered through booksellers or by contacting:

iUniverse
1663 Liberty Drive
Bloomington, IN 47403
www.iuniverse.com
1-800-Authors (1-800-288-4677)

ISBN: 978-1-5320-6361-9 (sc)
ISBN: 978-1-5320-6360-2 (e)

Library of Congress Control Number: 2018914044

Print information available on the last page.

iUniverse rev. date: 11/27/2018

Contents

Acknowledgements

To my children: Glenn B. Hester III (RIP), Christine Yarborough, Kimberly Hester, Karen Jones.

To my grandchildren: Jaime M. Tanner, Brianna Kichelle Hester (RIP), Ciera Yarborough, Tyrus Jones, Torrance Williams, Bryce Yarborough.

To my great grandchildren: Kyler Tanner, Paisley Tanner, Xander Tanner, Rowan Tanner.

Special thanks to Pam and Bob Hammer of PAMS No. 1 Law Enforcement Dinner Club in Glynco, Georgia.

Thanks to Dr. Jennifer Miller for finding the blockages in my arteries and saving my life.

Thanks to God for helping me get through this path and the obstacles endured.

Foreword

In the nineteenth century, British magician and prolific inventor John Nevil Maskelyne created a legendary stage illusion known as Metamorphosis. Later popularized by Harry Houdini, the illusion involves two people—one captive in a trunk, one free—switching places in the blink of an eye. Aside from being very clever and seemingly impossible, the illusion serves as a profound metaphor for the transformative and restorative power of art. As you will discover in these pages, magic entertains, but it also can educate and heal performer and spectator alike.

I have known Glenn Hester many years as a fellow magician and good friend. He has known and endured unimaginable personal loss, but you would never know it if you met him. He radiates positivity, compassion and generosity. Overcoming tragedy with the aid of friends, family and faith, he has dedicated his life to helping and protecting others. Glenn was able to combine his profession in law enforcement with his passion, magic, creating a unique niche for himself. Like Maskelyne and Houdini, who both exposed fraudulent spiritualists, Glenn uses his talents to expose carnival scams and con artists. It is an important public service.

A talented magician creates a rapport with the audience.

We are engaged, amazed. The impossible becomes possible; things disappear and reappear. It is captivating. Reading Glenn's story is similarly transporting. It's impossible not to be inspired by his journey and his true sense of mission.

In this moving and fascinating book, we accompany Glenn as he travels from tragedy to triumph, from the depths of despair to a renewed purpose. Along the way, we learn how to protect ourselves against fraud while gaining valuable insights into friendship and resilience. It is a journey you won't forget.

James Munton

Dedications

Fr. Cyprian Murray, ofm, cap.
Magic Ian Sutz
Robert Steiner

I met Fr. Cyprian when I was in the monastery in Garrison, New York in the early 1980's. He did some entertainment for the friars as well as use magic in his Homilies at Mass.

Fr. Cyprian, who was a Capuchin Franciscan Priest, was, at that time, Chaplain for the Society of American Magicians and later went on to become the president of the society. I hold a certificate he signed for me showing me as a certified magician.

Watching him turn a magic trick into a message was so cool to witness that I knew I wanted to use magic with messages to instill certain themes to others.

Fr. Cyprian taught me the use of props, sleight of hand and a certain style with people. His insight into magic was interesting and very helpful to my style.

I borrowed a book from the local library to learn all I could and used some of the tricks shown in the book to perform for the friars I lived with. I later purchased some props from magic dealers that helped me build my collection.

Sadly, not being that versed in magic props, I had to get rid of some that I felt I could not use.

Magic Ian Sutz owned a magic shop in the next county to mine when I was a deputy sheriff in Sullivan County, New York. My wife, Debbie, and I traveled to Middletown, New York to look over what he had for sale.

Ian was very helpful showing me the routine for each trick as well as showing me the secret to it. He also sponsored the Society of American Magicians Assembly and had monthly meetings at his magic shop as well as holding an annual contest for Magician of the Year.

I entered the contests and came in second that first year. The next year, I won first place doing a Gospel routine and a regular comedy routine for 1984-85. I left for Georgia to pursue law enforcement in my home state but kept in touch with Ian for magic supplies.

Ian moved to Florida later and designed a webpage for my Police Magic business. He also assisted with publishing my books on Lulu.com, a print on demand company.

He later made DVD's for the subject matter of each book where I showed crooked carnival games, some of the routines for my con game themes as well as some routines with my puppets and magic for Police Magic.

Ian also took a magic show for me on St. Simons Island, Georgia when I was not able to do it. He stayed with my girlfriend, Maria, and me and gave a bunch of magic props to my grandson, Jaime, who loved watching him perform.

Ian also invented some magic tricks which I used in my police magic routines and he authored several books to help magician's. Ian was a great help to me with the police magic routines and I will never forget his insight into using them.

He also wrote the Foreword and a chapter in the Police

Magician book on how to promote your shows and with whom you need to contact.

Robert Steiner was the former past president of the Society of American Magicians and a big promoter for the prevention of fraudulent health practices and bunco.

I contacted Bob in my early years and he was pleased to know how I used magic to promote crime prevention and educate the public on con games, crooked carnival games and show youth issues on Stranger Danger, drug addiction, personal safety and so on.

Bob and I finally met in Chicago during a convention on confidence crimes. I did a segment on using magic for bunco themes. Bob did a segment on psychic readings and psychic surgery.

Bob pulled a magician's trick to "randomly" choose a volunteer to assist him with his demonstration on psychic surgery. Once I got on the table, he proceeded to sterilize my stomach with a red dye water, which soaked my pants and underwear.

He then pulled a pencil from my stomach, and some diseased tissue that psychic surgeons display. Bob finished his presentation and we both went to the restroom to clean up. While he was washing his hands, I mentioned how wet he got my pants and underwear when he flooded me with the liquid.

He stated to put some paper towels in my pants and that should help. Right about that time, a conventioneer from another group exited the stall, looked at Bob washing the red off his hands, then looked at me with the red on my stomach.

He washed his hands quickly and left the restroom. However, curiosity got the best of him and he came up to Bob and me in the hallway and asked what the initials to our group, PACC, stood for. I made a joke and told him it was Proctologists Association of Central Chicago. PACC really stood for Professionals Against Confidence Crimes.

Bob wrote a book on Bunco that is still on the market today. It has some great info in it and he was a great help in formulating my Stranger Danger routine when the stranger grabs the child.

Bob and I conversed on the telephone many a night about life, bunco and other topics. I am honored to have his Bunco book, autographed, which I read from time to time. He also made some magic routines which I have used for my police magic series.

Sadly, all three are deceased now, but what they instilled in me helped formulate the magic and messages shown in the Police Magic shows.

Other books by Glenn Hester

Police Magician
Deceptive Performances
Carnival Cop

Can be purchased through Amazon.com. I would like to thank James Munton for helping me transfer my books to Amazon. He worked hard at getting the books on Amazon.

He is the co author of "The Con", How scams work, why you're vulnerable and how to protect yourself. He also does presentations on scams as well as educating youth on the dangers of being on the internet.

His book, "Cybersense" The 7 steps to keeping your kids safe online is a great book to teach the dangers of being on the internet and "think before you click", which is his motto for them.

James has been a great friend all these years and hosts a forum on Facebook known as the Magic Bistro. He also has a webpage, jamesmunton.com. You can acquire the books and get info about his speaking engagements from this site.

Introduction

"Do not go where the path may lead, go instead
where there is no path and leave a trail."
Ralph Waldo Emerson

My twin daughters, Kimberly and Karen, have often remarked to me how they would have loved to have known their older brother, Glenny. I told them on several occasions had Glenny not died, I would not have traveled the road that led me to their mother, and they would never been born.

You could say it all started on July 14, 1977. I was attending a birthday party at a restaurant on St. Simons Island, Georgia for my youngest sister, Joy. We had just finished dinner and were getting to dessert when I started to feel depressed.

The next day would have been my son, Glenny's, fourth birthday. My son was murdered on November 13, 1976 by my second wife, who was not his biological mother. She had already been convicted of murder in April of 1977 and was serving her sentence in prison.

I excused myself from the party, went to a liquor store and bought a bottle of bourbon. I parked my car and walked on the beach while consuming the contents of the alcoholic beverage. My heart was heavy, and my mind was thinking of my first-born child who was strangled and drowned by his stepmother. I looked at the ocean and contemplated walking into it to end my life.

As I started to go into the ocean, a voice in my head told me to stop as there were special plans for me in the future. To this day, I do not know if I really had a voice say that or if it was the product of my cowardice of being too scared to continue with my pursuit.

I decided not to go through with it and walked back onto the beach. I cried throughout that evening and stayed on the beach until I felt I could drive my vehicle. I went back to my parent's place and went to bed.

I thought a lot about that night on the beach and wondered just what plans were in store for me. Shortly after my son was murdered, I quit the job at the bank that my father was a large investor with. Prior to this, while I was married to my son's mother, I was a fireman in Americus, Georgia and loved life there. My son was born in Americus in July of 1973.

I left Americus to go back to Augusta, Georgia to learn about my father's business as he wanted me to take it over one day. Although I was not happy about this decision, I did it for my wife, Gail, and my son. This was one of the worse decisions I ever made.

To make a long story short, Gail and I later divorced. I got custody of my son through tough legal action which she did not deserve. I learned about surveying land then went to work at a bank my dad was involved with. At that time, my dad was wealthy and had a maid come help me with Glenny while I worked.

I dated a few women and met my soon to be second

wife at a mixer. Gloria was a legal secretary in my father's law firm. She was working for one of my dad's law partner's. We hit it off pretty well and started dating.

The bank was just across the street from the law office, so we had lunch and met for drinks after work at times. As our relationship grew, we contemplated getting married. Gloria was four years older than me but that did not bother me.

We got married in October of 1976. I bought a house just across the river in North Augusta, South Carolina. It needed some remodeling, so Glenny and I moved into her apartment and gave the townhouse, Glenny and I were staying in, back to my dad.

A little over a month after we were married, for whatever reason that she never told me, she killed my son. Life was a pure Hell after that and I was waking each day with anger and questions as to why this happened. Gloria died in 2002, never saying she was sorry for what she did or explaining why she did it.

I decided a few months later to move back to Americus and see about getting my old job back at the fire department. I felt that being in the city where life had been good and where my son was born would help me find the peace I so wanted as my heart ached each day.

I made a few trips back to Americus and finally moved back when the job came through.

Fire Department

After moving back to Americus, I purchased a house on Fulton Street that was in a nice neighborhood. It had a master bedroom with bath, a second bedroom, a full bath and a smaller bedroom that I made my study. I decorated it with fire memorabilia as I was back in the job I loved.

The schedule for the fire department was different this time around. Instead of working 24 hours on, 24 hours off and having a Kelly Day (an extra day off) after 8 days, we worked 24 hours on, 48 hours off and every Wednesday we would work an 8-hour shift. When we were off duty on a Monday, we could always check with one of the other firemen, who was your relief, and he could work a double on Wednesday, so you could have five days off.

I loved this work shift as each third week, I could have those extra days off. I did go back to work part time at Hancock Funeral Home, where I had worked part time when I first lived in Americus. So, the extra money made there also helped. By the way, Larry Hancock, the owner, was there for my son's birth, so I asked him to be there for my son in death. He was kind enough to travel to Augusta during this time and bring a casket to place my son in. Larry is now deceased.

I wanted to find peace as my heart was still heavy with the death of my son and I tormented over what could I have done to prevent this from happening. I went back to church and met a Franciscan priest, Fr. Anthony Moore, who was a great spiritual director. He and I hit it off and I found myself over at the rectory assisting him in his duties.

I sold my house to a police officer and moved in with one of my co-worker's mother who had a room available. I also stayed at the rectory at St. Mary's Catholic Church to help Fr. Anthony. He got calls from people who were contemplating suicide and I would drive him to those venues to assist the victim.

Fr. Anthony had other priests visiting but I will never forget one such priest that I was introduced too. His name was Fr. Anthony Schneider and was a missionary to Bolivia. This friar was a sleight of hand magician who showed me marvelous feats of dexterity with coins and cards.

I learned all I could while he visited Fr. Anthony and took an interest in magic. I practiced with the coins and cards and learned what I could after he left. I had to work in front of a mirror, so I could see what the audience would see and learn to be natural in my moves.

Fr. Anthony was a frequent visitor at the fire hall when I was on duty. I was pleased to see how he was received by the other members of the department as they were mostly of protestant faith. Fr. Anthony wore his habit all the time and was even received by President Jimmy Carter's mother, "Miss Lillian" in Plains, Georgia. He had a great personality and people loved him.

I witnessed a lot of what he did for people as a Franciscan and wondered what it would be like to live that kind of life. Fr. Anthony knew my history and what had happened to my son. He counseled me on my anger and hate for the woman who killed Glenny, but I still harbored those feelings toward her.

After a while, he was convinced that I might make a good "Franciscan Brother" in his order, so he contacted the vocation director in Bronx, New York. I made plans to visit them for a week and go over details of the life while meeting others who were of the same mindset.

During this transition, Fr. Anthony was reassigned to another parish in upstate New York. My best friend on the fire department, Ricky Traywick, and I drove Fr. Anthony to the airport to fly up to New York and say goodbye. It was a sad day as I knew I would miss him. He did continue to work on my moving to his order while he was in another parish.

We came up with a plan for me to move to Callicoon, New York and work with Fr. Anthony in his parish until his order was ready for me to join them. I had a lot to do to get ready for this. I had to pay off any debts, sell my car and set a date for my resignation from the fire department.

While this was going on, three job offers happened that almost got me to renege on going up North. One was working with the state fire marshal's office investigating arson. One was working for the state firemen's association of Georgia and the last one, which I almost took, was being promoted to a lieutenant and working on fire prevention as I had already done a lot of work on this over the last two years that proved successful.

I also had to take medical and psychological testing with the Franciscans. After all that was done, Fr. Anthony told the vocation director his plans to have me come live in the parish in Callicoon to get a taste of the life of a friar. The vocation director said that would be helpful to be a postulant for awhile there before coming with them.

As I thought I was a shoo in with the friars, I embarked on getting things ready to make the move. My best friend,

Ricky, and I flew up to Callicoon to stay with Fr. Anthony for a while, so I could see what it was like up there. It was during the winter and we were delayed getting there due to a snow storm. We finally made it the next day after having to stay overnight in another city where we got snowed in.

I liked what I saw when I got there. We were greeted by the members of the church and loved the snow all over the place. This was a new experience for two Southern boys as snow in the trees and on the ground is not a common site in the South. Before departing, I set a date for Fr. Anthony to drive down to my hometown of Augusta, Georgia where he could pick me up at my parent's house.

I returned to Americus, put my resignation in and worked on driving back to Augusta to meet Fr. Anthony. My parents were thrilled with the decision I had made as my dad was a very devoted Catholic and knew just how sinful I was over the years.

It was very sad for me to leave Americus as many memories I held were in that city. I loved my job as a fireman and part time work at the funeral home. I also lived at the funeral home for a while to keep down expenses, so I could make the move to New York.

The day I left Americus, I stopped by an old pub to have one last meal there. My car was loaded up with a couple of footlockers and suitcases that held my life in them. I had given most of my fire books to the chief of the fire department and some others to the local library. I also gave away many of the fire memorabilia that I treasured.

I said goodbye to Americus and drove to Augusta to await Fr. Anthony's arrival to pick me up and begin a new life that I hoped would find me peace and contentment.

The Monkery

I often joked and called the monastery the monkery as many people called the priests and brothers monks instead of friars. I was somewhat nervous about this move in my life as it was a new experience and I wondered how I would do with it. I also knew how much I liked women and wondered if I could go without sex for the rest of my life as you take vows to obey the church and order, poverty, where you cannot own anything of your own and chastity, where you must remain pure and not have sexual relations.

I arrived in Augusta and stayed with my parents for a couple of days until Fr. Anthony arrived to pick me up. This gave me time to say goodbye to my family. When Fr. Anthony arrived, he stayed overnight, and we left the next day after loading up his car.

It was somewhat a shock to see the discipline he put me through once we arrived. I was no longer a care free man. I had to follow the rule of St. Francis and act in a certain manner to all those I encountered. I was forbidden to reveal my past about my son or be as earthy as I normally was around people. This was hard to change, but I endured it. I learned the history of the Franciscans and the order of Friars Minor. Fr. Anthony said mass each day during the week with us going through the ritual of reciting the office of hours several times during the day and evening. This was a spiritual reading from the books we had that helped us maintain the religious way of life.

I decided to grow a beard since Fr. Anthony had a couple of habits (Franciscan robes) made for me. It did not have the hood on it as he only inducted me into the Third Order of St. Francis Secular. I did have the rope around my waist with the three knots to symbolize the three vows I would be taking. This was a lot different than I had imagined.

After about four months, Fr. Anthony got a call from the vocation director. He was told that the psychological exam showed scarring from the death of my son and the psychologist thought I was running away to escape the pain I felt. In a sense, I was joining to attempt to find peace and contentment, but I was not running away from my problems. I still had anger issues and hatred toward the woman who killed my son but had hoped this lifestyle would divest me of this feeling over time.

At the end of the phone call, Fr. Anthony broke the news to me. His order decided I should wait a few years before joining so the pain could subside. I reminded him that the vocation director said he had no problem with me moving up here as a postulant until I could join the order. Now, what could I do since I got rid of all my stuff and left a great career behind?

Fr. Anthony confided in a classmate of his who was a priest at another parish down the road. Fr. Raymond knew of a psychologist priest in Larchmont, New York who as at Trinity Retreat. Although this was another Franciscan order (Capuchins), it was still a Franciscan family. He made plans for all of us to drive there and see Fr. Benedict. I was still reeling from the news of the vocation director but said I would go and see what could be done.

We arrived at Trinity Retreat and met with Fr. Benedict. I shook his hand and he said that I had anger issues. However, we sat down and discussed joining the Capuchin Franciscans. I was still angry about the rejection to the Order of Friars Minor but cooled down and listened to what Fr. Benedict had to say.

Fr. Anthony and Fr. Benedict worked together to get me started on the process of being in the Capuchin Franciscans. Fr. Benedict stated that I could come and live at Trinity Retreat and work with him during that time until the novitiate. The novitiate is a year and a day in the monastery where you are trained and evaluated before taking simple vows.

Fr. Benedict did my psychological testing and said that I did have anger issues from the death of my son, but those could be addressed and worked on. Here was a friar who had some faith in me, like Fr. Anthony. I continued working and living with Fr. Anthony until the designated time that I would move to Larchmont at Trinity Retreat. During that time, I had to make a few visits there to get acclimated to the transition of being a Capuchin. When the time came, Fr. Anthony drove me to Trinity Retreat where I was given a room, a Franciscan smock and told what my duties would be. I met with other members of the staff there and hit it off great with Brother Bob, who was the chef for the house.

My assignment, when I was not working around the house, was to drive Fr. Benedict to his conferences where he gave spiritual lectures to the masses of people attending. I did not know he was such a celebrity until I attended his lectures and saw the reverence given him. He was a great public speaker and used humor in his presentations.

This was a style I adapted in my messages using magic. No matter how serious a theme was, I always injected humor in it to liven it up a bit. And I have Fr. Benedict to thank for showing me that it could be done. Driving Fr. Benedict to his lectures, and having the honor of listening to him, was an experience I will never forget.

While at Trinity Retreat, I met a man who authored books on poems. He wanted to write a book on the Patron Saint of Fire Fighters, Saint Florian. Having been a fireman, I thought this would be great. I did research at the seminary in Yonkers, New York and got the information needed for the book. It was published while I was a Novice at the monastery in Garrison, New York. The book is titled, "The Book of Florian" Patron Saint of Fire Fighters, by William Foley. I am pleased to have been a part of this book, which started my literary career.

One incident that sticks with me is when we went to Manhattan to pick up Donna Summer, the famous singer who was married to the brother of one of our friars. She rode with us to meet Mother Teresa of Calcutta to donate to her work house. Donna was a born again Christian and wanted to know how a Southern boy like me wanted to become a monk. I jokingly put on my best Jerry Falwell accent and told her "Sister, listen", and described why I wanted to become a Capuchin Franciscan Friar.

We arrived at the work house of the Sisters of Charity in the South Bronx where she witnessed the work they did with the poor. After that we went to the contemplative house where Mother Teresa was and sat on the floor. I sat next to Mother Teresa and her advice to me was to persevere in my vocation. I will never forget this experience as long as I live.

I continued working with Fr. Benedict until time to enter the novitiate at Garrison, New York. Fr. Anthony picked me up and drove me to the monastery in Garrison where I met many of those in my class. There was one guy who was older than me, but all the others were much younger. We got settled in our cells (room) and told the rules of the house. The next day, we were vested with our habits. I still have a picture of me receiving the habit and the picture of us after we donned it. The habit is the brown robe that symbolizes you are preparing for death.

Living and working there was a great experience. We had classes, manual labor, meals and outside activities that we were expected to do. I taught a CYO in Buchanan, New York and visited the elderly at a nursing home on certain days. I also went to the local library to borrow a book on magic that showed some impromptu tricks as well as learning the methods magicians used to achieve the effect of the tricks.

I was able to attain some professional magic props from magic dealers from money my mother sent me at times. I put on a magic show for the friars in our monastery and loved it. I also met with Fr. Cyprian Murray and he helped me formulate my style. As mentioned in the dedication, Fr. Cyprian showed me how to use magic to get a message across, so I worked on Gospel Magic messages as well.

One part of living together that I did not care for was the getting together each Tuesday for wine and cheese. First, I did not care for cheese and did not drink wine. I did not mind the feast days or birthday celebrations but felt meeting for a "Sorsum Corda" each week took away from those celebrations. That was a strike against me for evaluation.

During this period, the friars in charge of us evaluated each of us to see if we measured up to the standards for being Capuchin Franciscans. I was blunt with my words as I did not hold back if something bothered me. I also used profanity at times that "slipped" out of my mouth.

There was one friar there that I was not too happy with. He oversaw the kitchen and other jobs that was expected of the non-clerical brother. He had me cook dinner for the friars one Sunday evening while he had a day off. He may not have cared for me either as he had to shop for the food and one item on it was Grits. Had it been just me, he would not have gotten them, but a priest there liked them and told him to get double the order for me as well.

The next morning, I was in the refectory (dining room) drinking coffee when this friar approached me and asked about the dinner last night. I told him there were no left overs and everyone seemed to enjoy it. He asked about the potatoes I made. I told him that I made a mistake on them and made boiled instead of baked. Well, he took exception to it and made his mind known about it.

I apologized and thought that would be it until he started up again. I apologized one more time and he started up again. I lost my cool at this point. We got into a confrontation and I had to go see the Father Superior about it. When asked what the problem was with this friar, I said some things that were not nice, using profanity toward the friar. I was told I had an anger problem. I said I had a Brother (I won't mention his name) problem. I explained that where I come from, you apologize once and that is it. I swallowed my pride and apologized twice but would not a third time and that is when the confrontation began.

I thought things had settled down after that but later, when the friars met to do evaluations, I found out they dismissed me from the order. It was heartbreaking to call Fr. Anthony and tell him the bad news as he had wanted me to make it. After a few days, Fr. Anthony came to pick me up and take me back to Callicoon.

While I was contemplating what to do with my life now, I met a woman in Callicoon who I took a shine too. She was a single mother with a young daughter who lived above the pharmacy where she worked. I bought a briefcase from her at the store and we spent time together. I started having feelings for her but wanted to check out one more thing before I made a commitment.

I investigated going into another order and planned to visit the Benedictines in St. Leo, Florida. This was a monastic order that lived and died at the monastery, never traveling around to other parishes. Fr. Benedict had spoken with the Abbot there and sent a letter to him about me. The Abbot spoke with me upon my arrival and introduced me to a monk who used to be a Baptist who turned Catholic turned Monk.

I stayed a week at the monastery to see their way of life. They were going to allow me to keep my magic props, work with children, be known as Brother Florian (patron saint of fire fighters) as you could change to a Saints name. Everything I wanted was going to be given to me.

Then, on the last day, the Abbot called me into his office and asked how I liked the lifestyle. I told him I was impressed but did not like not being able to travel. He told me that was one of the disciplines that I would have to endure. He told me to think about this week, pray over it and get back with him later with my answer. One last thing he told me was to think about what I would be happy with ten years from now. I gave it a lot of thought and realized that I wanted to start up a relationship with the woman who lived in Callicoon.

I moved back to Callicoon and started to look for a job in the area.

Magician

I moved into the Western Hotel in Callicoon when I got back from Florida and told Fr. Anthony that my plans for religious life would not be realized. He was saddened by this but understood that I would not have my heart in it.

My mother sent me money from a bond she cashed in and I purchased many magic tricks that I could use for birthday parties and other events to make some money. I also found employment at a local hotel in the area that had me bell hopping and driving the bus for guests. This helped earn a living, but I wanted to expand on my magic.

I talked with the general manager and asked him if I could do magic shows at the hotel for the guests. He auditioned me and found I had talent. He allowed me to do shows for the senior citizens who were guests there. Word got back to him how much the guests enjoyed my show, so I was put on once a week to entertain the people. One woman told me that she enjoyed my style as all the other magicians she saw were crude and rude to the audience. I was given my moniker by her. She called me a "Southern Gentleman". That name stuck with me and I had business cards made up showing the Magic of Glenn Hester, The Southern Gentleman.

During the Summer I did the children's shows as well as the senior citizens along with driving the bus and bell hopping. I was also dating Debbie, who I had fallen in love with. She still worked at the pharmacy and lived upstairs with her daughter, Christine. As much as I liked doing the magic and driving the bus, I knew this lifestyle would not be much on supporting a family, especially if we were to have other children.

It just so happened that an article in our local town newspaper about my style of magic was caught by the publisher of that newspaper. He knew my work with children when I was known as "Brother Glenn" working with the CYO and Fr. Anthony. I was also the driver for President Carter's mother, Miss Lillian, when she came to Callicoon to break ground for the new church and again a year later to help dedicate it. The publisher suggested I should go to work for the sheriff's office and work with the youth division. I had thought about law enforcement as a career in my younger days but now this could become a reality.

I continued doing magic shows for special events, birthday parties, school functions and the hotel until I was called to meet the sheriff of Sullivan County.

I told his secretary that I had a show that afternoon at the hotel but could come after that if he wanted. She said that would be good and we decided on a time. After the show, I traveled to Monticello, New York and met the sheriff.

He told me that Fred Stabbert, Jr. had spoken highly of me and thought I would be an asset to the sheriff's office working with the youth. The sheriff told me that he had no openings in the youth division but could start me as a deputy sheriff working in the jail and working my way up.

We had a great meeting and got the paperwork done for my employment with the Sullivan County Sheriff's Office. While I was awaiting on the date to start, Debbie and I planned our wedding. We moved into an upstairs apartment above a store in Callicoon and fixed it up to our liking. It was at this time that I was notified of my start date with the sheriff's office and the salary I would receive.

Debbie and I were married on August 15, 1983 in Afton, New York at the home of her parents. Her daughter, Christine, was in the bridal party. My parents attended, and it was a great wedding. We had a lot of fun at the reception prior to the wedding and the honeymoon at the hotel in Chenago County was even better.

Ten days from now, I thought, I would be a deputy sheriff. Things were looking up for me now and I knew I could support my family. I still had magic shows in the area with special events, the hotels and other venues so that would be extra money to help. Debbie got a job at the local bank where she advanced to Head Teller. A friend of ours allowed us to move into their apartment in Hortonville, New York, just down the road from Callicoon.

I started thinking about Fr. Cyprian and how he used magic with messages in his spiritual sermons and wondered if I could transfer Gospel Magic into law enforcement themes for youth and adults. I wanted to be set apart from the stereotyped magician who just does the entertainment. I wanted to educate and entertain.

I started working on some routines with the tricks I had in my collection.

Sheriff's Office

Starting with the sheriff's office involved several days of training before I could be cut loose. More paperwork had to be finished, qualifications with a firearm and the use of force training was a big part of it. Understanding what my job description was and the state laws I would have to enforce after I graduated the police academy were a big part of it.

I finally got into the academy and finished on the job training with a training deputy. For a good part of the two years working in the jail, I worked the tiers and visiting room. An opening came up for protective detail on court security. I was reassigned to work the county court. The deputy who used to work county court had been transferred to Family Court but wanted to come back to county court, so we switched places.

Family Court was an emotional court as the lives of children and parents were affected by the decisions of the judge. Sometimes, I had to take juveniles into custody and transport them to secure detention facilities when the judge ordered it. Being in this court gave me an opportunity to use some of the magic with a message to calm the people down and present messages on how to be better citizens, anti-drug, peer pressure and personal safety.

It was also during this time that I could work with the lieutenant of the Youth Division, Richard Bliss, when he had to do lectures and presentations to the public. He allowed me to accompany him on many details and I did magic on home security, Neighborhood Watch and other issues of crime prevention, which went over well.

I also made a couple of trips to the Sheriffs Summer Ranch where children from around the state were sent for a week to mingle with other law enforcement personnel to learn about their duties. The first year I attended, I did a 45-minute show on issues pertaining to the youth.

I had about ten routines on issues of anti-drug, peer pressure, obeying rules and laws, consequences of breaking the law, good citizenship and a few more. I got to know some of the children and a couple of Christine's friends attended each of those two years.

The second year was even better. I had improved on the amount of routines I could show the youth and made a few that dealt with good citizenship and Stranger Danger. At the end of the week, the night prior to us leaving, one child, who I thought would turn out to be a problem, gave testimony on how my attitude and magic made an impression on him and he wanted to be a better person because of it. Tears came to my eyes as he came over to hug me.

I was able to do statewide presentations to other groups after the sheriff got a great letter from the sheriff's association on my shows. The association also did an article about the presentations which is in my portfolio today. The local CSEA Union did an article on my Police Magic later which was received by many law enforcement agencies. Prior to moving back to Georgia, I was hired to instruct several agencies near the capitol by Albany, New York.

I did a segment on a local television show in Kingston,

New York that introduced people to a couple of routines I used, and the messages shown. The first one showed me making a red scarf vanish, which symbolized the child, and making it appear in a fully inflated clear balloon, which symbolized a jail. I then pulled the scarf out of the fully inflated balloon showing this will not occur if they stay a model citizen.

The next routine was showing the addiction to drugs. I had the host lock my wrists with chains attached to an oval ring. She then covered my hands. I explained how being addicted to alcohol or drugs trapped a person. At that time, I released one of my hands and brought it out in front of the cloth covering my hands. Then I put it back under the cloth.

The host was surprised and questioned me about it. I told her that I released my hand to show how many think drugs or alcohol is an escape, but, they are still trapped. That is when I showed both hands still secured by the chains. She was amazed with that. I then proceeded to explain that saying no to drugs or alcohol keeps the person free to enjoy their life and then showed both hands free of the bonds of the shackles.

The host was overwhelmed with both routines and questioned me further than the segment was to air. I was pleased to talk about the other routines I performed and what their messages showed. Being this was a taped interview for a future date, I mentioned an upcoming appearance with the New York State Catholic Youth Organization for the New York Dioceses in another venue.

I got a copy of this interview which I love to watch sometimes to show how awkward I was on my first televised program. I did a little better on the next one. Judge Anthony Kane, the Family Court judge for Sullivan County, and I did a presentation on family court and the messages I showed with Police Magic. I used the same two tricks and messages as I did with the first show as it was shown in another county that was three counties away from the first televised interview I did.

I started writing a book on the routines after speaking with Fr. Cyprian over the phone. I wanted others to learn about this and use them. I talked to Francis Marshal in Chicago about it and an article was printed in the Linking Ring, a publication of the International Brotherhood of Magicians, about it. I was going to call the book "Sheriffs Safety Show".

These television presentations as well as the printed media helped give me the exposure I wanted to do more shows. I was hired by a couple of other resorts in the Catskills to do once a week shows for their guests as well as appearances at other venues where people went to vacation. This proved profitable for me when not working as a deputy sheriff during the day. Most were in the evenings or at night.

Also, during this time, my wife was pregnant with twin girls. We expected their arrival in February of 1987, but they came nine weeks early. Kimberly was two pounds, ten ounces and Karen was three pounds, two ounces when birthed. They had to stay at the hospital for two months, so they could gain the weight needed to be brought home.

This early delivery put a damper on our finances as my wife could not work, therefore reducing the income for the household. Thankfully, those once a week magic shows, along with the extra shows given, made up for the loss and kept our head above water. All this while my wife and I drove back and forth from our place in Hortonville, New York to Scranton, Pennsylvania at the Neo Natal unit.

Finally, we were able to get ready to bring them home. Kim had not gained a full five pounds like her twin sister, Karen. Kim also had to be brought home on an apnea bra cardia monitor as she sometimes stopped breathing and her heart rate lowered. We went through first aid and other courses for premature children prior to the hospital releasing the children to us.

During the two months that my twin daughters were recovering in the neo natal unit, I did some magic for the nurses to entertain them. One of the nurses had to question us on certain things we needed to know. She asked my wife what the difference was between an oral and rectal thermometer. Debbie answered correctly. Then, I was asked how I tell the difference between them. I told the nurse that I would sniff it.

This got a laugh from the nurse, but my wife hit me and said if I did not take this seriously they would not allow our daughters to come home with us. I reminded her how much the bill was for their birth and care these past two months. It was over 200 thousand dollars and still climbing.

The night before we were to take the twins home, we had to share a room with them at the hospital. The monitor Kim wore did go off a few times, but she was alright. The next day, we loaded the twins in the car seats and took them to their new home. It was an adventure having them. I worked all day as a deputy sheriff in family court, did magic shows once a week at various resorts in the area as well as driving the bus for the hotel.

This took a lot out of me and the bags under my eyes were getting bigger by the day. My poor wife had the twins during the day until Christine got home from school and Christine helped her mom until I got home. My parents came up to visit their grandchildren and witnessed how tired and run down we all were. I told my dad I would not trade it for anything as these little ones went through much more just to survive.

I later found out that the insurance company the county had for me paid out 80 percent of the bill. I had to pay 20 percent of it. My wife could not go back to work as she had to be with the twins to take care of them. Doctors' offices and others in the medical profession, who were responsible for the care of my twin daughters, called to ask about payment on their bill. I told them I was doing what I could and to be patient.

Thankfully, the jobs I had brought in more than both of us made when Debbie was working at the bank. I watched the twins grow and develop and had such a great time bonding with them. I think Christine liked the idea of having sisters as well. We were a family and I wanted to do the best I could for all of them. Well, another wrench was thrown at me.

The insurance company the county used for the sheriff's office notified me that I had exceeded my limit and was no longer going to be covered. I wondered how I could take care of my family without health insurance. My sister in Brunswick, Georgia knew a lieutenant at the county police department who I corresponded with about employment there. I made a few visits, met with the chief of police and showed him some of what I could offer the county police department in Glynn County.

He liked the television show I did in Kingston, New York where the two routines were shown to the host. The training division lieutenant watched it as well and was amazed with what I could do. This was a great public relations gimmick for the department. We spoke about the job requirements there and what all I would have to go through once hired.

At that time, the police academy was in Brunswick and only six weeks long. The chief thought I may be able to skip a few courses since I had already been through it in New

York, but I told him I would like to do the full six weeks. I made application and had to return a couple of more times for the aptitude testing as well as the physical testing.

As fate would have it, prior to my taking the physical testing, I had a problem with an ingrown hair in my rectum. It caused me pain and I could not have bowel movements as the swelling was too intense. I had to have emergency surgery to get better. My wife thought I was going to the hospital to get out of being at her yard sale. She was surprised and felt bad for me when she got the call that I was being wheeled into the operating room for emergency surgery. Boy, did I feel great telling her, "I told you so", when she came to visit me during my recovery.

Thankfully, I had sick time on the books with the sheriff's office and the resorts understood my health issue so that was not a problem while I recovered. The judge of family court was great as he worked with me as well.

I had to go back to Brunswick twice. Once for the aptitude testing and the physical battery of testing. I was not fully recovered from the rectal surgery when I went through the physical battery and it showed. I barely made it in the time frame allotted as the pain of running, lifting, agility and other tests put a strain on me.

I returned to Sullivan County and resumed my work schedule until I heard from the chief. A few weeks went by and he wanted me to come in for an interview, so I made plans to go back to Brunswick and finish that. He said that would be the last stage before the psychological examination. He scheduled both the interview and psychological exam back to back, so I did not have to make an extra trip, which I appreciated very much as I had already taken a great deal of time off to complete this.

The interview went well and the next day I was scheduled

to go to Savannah, Georgia to speak with the doctor who was to administer the psychological exam. I learned something that I never knew after the exam. I had a learning disability that I never knew existed. All my life, especially in school, I had a hard time reading and comprehending what was taught in the books as I had to re-read it two or three times to grasp the thought.

This showed me I was not a dumbass like I thought I was before. I had a legitimate cause for not getting the information the first time around. Because of this disability, I pushed myself to be a self-starter and exceed my limits on various things. This caused me to do my best with magic, my job and other things that I encountered. I hated reading because of this disability but had to learn to adjust to it and take it in stride.

I felt better about myself and my self-esteem, which was so low, started to improve. I honed my talents and skills on magic and the jobs I had with more confidence. I started working on routines for adults on bunco themes where I showed how many con games used principles of magic to get the scam across.

I met another magic cop through the Society of American Magicians magazine. Bruce Walstad had placed an article in the classified section of the magazine. I contacted him and told him what I did with certain magic tricks showing bunco themes. We became fast friends after that and kept in touch.

Bruce wrote his first book, "Sting Shift", with his partner, Lindsay Smith. It was a book about various con games played on unsuspecting victims. Bruce gave me a copy since he had mentioned me in the book. I was impressed. I joined his organization, Professionals Against Confidence Crimes. Bruce is retired now and does public speaking, lectures and seminars on a host of topics. His "Street Smart

Communications" business is known to many law enforcement agencies around the nation. More on Bruce later.

I got the news that I was accepted to join the Glynn County Police and they wanted me to start on July 25, 1988. This gave me about three months to find lodging in Brunswick for my family, make plans to get our household goods down there and take care of any unfinished business in New York.

Thankfully, my sister, Beannie, helped me with some of the things needed. Prior to leaving, I got a call from an officer near Albany, New York, who read the article in the CSEA newspaper about the Police Magic I did. He wanted me to come up and take a couple of days instructing a few officers from different agencies on this unique program.

I planned to do so and to cut costs, stayed with one of the officers at his apartment. I instructed the two days on how to use magic with messages for crime, drug and bunco prevention themes. I told the officers that I would like them to attempt a presentation the next day using one of the themes I showed them.

This was my first time instructing anyone on this and it was hit and miss but went well the two days. The first day was a little rocky start but I got into it by just being unconventional, unorthodox and animated, like I normally would be in a show. This made me, as well as the others, feel more comfortable. That night, the class went to a pub where we met for dinner and drinks.

Questions from the class were asked and answered during dinner and some more magic was show to them. After a good night's rest, the second day began. It was a little better as most of the routines had already been shown to the officers and that left them with a half day of finishing up the remainder of the class before we did the presentations.

Each officer selected one of the routines to present with their own patter. I was impressed with several of them as they presented the theme chosen as if they had been doing it for years. Others did a fair job as confidence was an issue with them but overall, they all were judged to have done a job well done.

I stayed one more night and left early the next day as I had to get back to work. My wife and I had to prepare things to move to Brunswick. Airline reservations were made for my wife, mother in law and the twins. Christine and her friend, Kristen, would ride with me along with our neighbor, Scott, who helped with the loading and unloading and driving the car behind the moving van that I drove.

I put my resignation in with the sheriff's office and told the judge of family court that I was moving back to my home state to work in law enforcement. He and the staff had my wife and I join them for a farewell dinner in Monticello. I hated leaving his court as he made it feel like a family. I resigned from the Sullivan County Sheriffs office and worked that week on securing a van and loading it with our household items. Scott was a big help with that. Debbie and her mother were leaving the next day on an airplane to Brunswick. They were going to stay in a motel in Brunswick until we arrived to get the keys to our new apartment that I visited prior to our leaving.

We had one overnight stay just less than halfway to Brunswick, so we could arrive at a decent hour. Once we arrived that afternoon and I pulled into the complex where my wife, Debbie, her mother and the twins were already there with my parents, sister and brother in law. It took a while to unload and set up the apartment. Christine, Kim and Karen would take the master bedroom with bath and Debbie and I would take the spare bedroom.

I went to the county police department to check on my status and was told that July 25th was the date to start my employment. I filled out my new address with them and looked forward to beginning a new career.

County Police Officer

As was the routine with the sheriff's office, I had to go through certain training with the Glynn County Police Department. I was given the Standard Operating Procedures books, a criminal code book, firearms qualification and uniforms.

Since I did 25 years with this agency, I will stick to the 11 years I did with the administration division except for four years prior to my retirement when my grand daughter was murdered.

After two years of doing patrol, the chief wanted to send me to the Drug Abuse Resistance Education (D.A.R.E.) training to educate fifth graders on the dangers of drugs. It was an experience being at that two-week training seminar.

I used a magic trick when we were to do a few minutes speech with our group. Each officer had to present something that was interesting and kept the attention of the group. I liked the officer who showed how to make a "mater sandwich". His presentation was humorous and made me hungry. My presentation consisted of a utility prop and red silk handkerchief. I made the silk vanish and reappear during my presentation which baffled all in attendance.

Most magicians will know the secret to this trick, so I won't reveal it here. This type assignment would prove to be a different style for me, but I was looking forward to educating the young people about the dangers of drugs since I already did this using the magic tricks in my police magic shows.

Teaching the DARE Program for 11 years was great. We focused on the fifth graders with the lesson plans but were given the opportunity to visit the other lower grades as well. This gave me a chance to use some of the police magic routines to entertain and educate the kindergarten through fourth grades.

I also did special events around the area. One such event was at our local mall. We had a display up with one of our slick top police cars parked by it. The other officer wore the McGruff costume at certain times and we had the children go through a traffic safety obstacle to learn about crossing the streets. My twin daughters and niece, Danielle, sat on the trunk of the police car during one of these events and loved the McGruff figure. It was at this time I met another magician who also did juggling, balloon sculptures and ventriloquism.

Cliff Patton was doing balloon sculptures for the children during this event and I made it a point to meet him. We hit it off as we talked about magic and what I did with the messages on crime and drug prevention. Cliff also did a puppet show with Skeeter. I loved watching the comedy and style he had during his presentation. Cliff was a great ventriloquist and entertained the masses who watched his show.

As time went on, Cliff and I kept in touch as he came down often to our area to do shows at local resorts. Over the years, Cliff stayed at our place when he had presentations in the area. He was also helpful showing me how to use a puppet for presentations. This gave me an idea to start using puppets for my children's Stranger Danger program. Our department had a McGruff the Crime Dog puppet that was not being used. Although it came with a program to use with the puppet, I decided to use it for the Stranger Danger routine as well as other issues on crime prevention since television showed him with PSA's. Thankfully I could speak like him so that was good.

I used this puppet for the school's lower grades when I did the DARE Program at the schools. Seeing how the children reacted to the puppet, the messages and antics, I thought this would be a great way to entertain and educate them. Although I was not as good as Cliff with lip control, I made the puppet animated enough where they would not concern themselves with my moving mouth.

Over the years, this was a great program, but I wanted something more personal. I did a program for a radio station where they would purchase a pig puppet for me. I told them I wanted to dress it in our uniform and do the programs I already do with the children. This way, I would not have to worry about copyrighted material using McGruff. Cliff knew a man who made puppets, so I contacted him, sent him a small pair of pants and a shirt that resembles our uniform, along with shoulder patches. I also put a badge, name plate and campaign type hat on it.

My chief allowed me to have an ID card made for it as well. Finally, a belt with a toy gun, handcuffs, radio and baton were put around the waist. This gave me the chance to speak on gun safety to the children, so they would not get hurt or killed if they came upon a weapon in their home or on the street. The hardest part was coming up with a voice for the pig puppet.

I use a Mortimer Snerd and Goofy type voice for it that allowed me to be able to sing a certain song at times. The name I chose for the puppet was "Patrolman Potbelly Pigg". Having his police ID was a great idea to show the children how to identify a real police officer from one that used a fake ID. The chief loved this and allowed me to do other functions with the pig puppet.

I continued instructing the DARE Program during the school year and sometimes went back on patrol during the Summer months or they would have me doing special assignments in the training division. I was sent to Savannah, Georgia to go through the Peace Officers Standards and Training for Instructor, so I could do in house training as well as instruct at the police academies around the state.

I had already self-published a book on Police Magic in 1992 that included an outline on con games. I thought instructing this course at our police academy in Forsyth, Georgia at the Georgia Public Safety Training Center would be a great way to get other officers to use these methods. I did a three-day course at the GPSTC and had a friend of mine who worked for the Brunswick Police department assist me. Bob May was also a DARE officer with his agency.

The course went over great. One of the officers in the class was the daughter of a fireman I used to work with in Americus. I remember using a remote-control fart machine in the class as a joke and showing them how it worked. They all loved it. One problem with dining at the cafeteria there is the food gave me a horrible case of the "winds". During class that afternoon, I accidently seeped out some gas that had a smell to it. One of the officers said that they knew how the fart machine worked but wanted to know how I got the smell with it. I told them it was a chemical I used to make it smell like the real thing. Thankfully, they bought that excuse.

After the three-day class, which I modeled on the two-day class done when I was in New York, I looked at the lesson plans put together and decided to rewrite the book on police magic. I renamed it Police Magician and put the section of using puppets in it as well. Magic Ian wrote a chapter on how to book the shows and who to contact for promotions. Ian used my manuscript to publish it with Lulu.com, a print on demand company. He also sold copies via my webpage, that he designed, and made it into an e-book as well.

I included routines on con games for the adult lectures to increase the amount of routines. I also did some magic showing carnival game fraud issues. I felt this would expand the Police Magic series as it showed fraud and bunco themes that could be presentations as well.

I had the opportunity to attend classes on bunco with Bruce Walstad. Bruce was instructing classes on con games and carnival game fraud at a college in Florida. I put in a request to attend these classes and was granted permission from the chief. I used a departmental vehicle and credit card to pay for the expenses.

The first day we learned about the different types of scams that were played on unsuspecting victims. I was amazed at all the different scams that were being played to con people. There were scams for people who wanted to do their civic duty, for people who came upon found money, home repair, telemarking as well as the gangs who did the shell and pea and three card monte.

Being a magician, I was able to use the principles of magic to perform the shell and pea and three card monte sleights. Bruce widened my knowledge about the flim-flam on the streets, in the stores when the cashier would get taken by change raising or get scammed the customer by giving back incorrect and less change. He also showed paranormal phenomenal type frauds that fortune tellers did. I loved learning about this type fraud as I could use some magic with this theme.

The days that followed showed the different games on the midway that would give the player little or no chance of winning. As I knew something was amiss when I attended certain carnivals and played the games, I longed to learn the secrets of how I was scammed. Although I doubt the carnival game agents knew the principles used, it was shown that the laws of physics, principles of science and magic were part of many of the games.

This gave me an idea about inspecting the games at our local fair and those carnivals that set up shop in the parking lots of our businesses in my area. However, I would need others to have this knowledge. I thought about having Bruce come to our area and put on a small seminar with our agency as well as our vice squad and have some people from the sponsoring club attend to witness what had been happening with mischief on the midway.

It would be awhile before I could do this as there was no cause to do it at this time. About a year or so later, the president of the sponsoring club came to me and told me that one of the citizens was ripped off for about three hundred dollars at a crooked game at their fair. I told him that I was about to go to another seminar on carnival game fraud and would see if I could get the instructor to come up and do a presentation on it for us.

I got the ball rolling by getting two police organizations to foot the expenses for Bruce to do this. Then, I notified the chiefs of both my agency and the city agency as well as the vice squad and president of the sponsoring organization. It was all set prior to my attending a second class on this down in Florida. Bruce would follow me back to Brunswick, stay at my house to keep expenses down, set his equipment up in our training room and instruct the next day.

I had the local newspaper attend to witness the class, so the citizens would know we were looking out for them. This had pros and cons. Many liked it, but some, in the club that sponsored the event, thought it made them look like they were in on the scam. I assured them that the objective would be to show the organization is working to make it fair to patrons that attend this event.

Bruce put on a great presentation which gave the knowledge needed to our officers and agents. We showed the three members of the local club sponsoring the fair how some of the games could rip a patron off. The newspaper reporter took some pictures and did a great article on what our agencies were doing to make the local fair honorable. I got a lot of good reviews from this although some still held the belief that all the games on the midway were crooked.

Preparations were made to notify the owner of the carnival that our agency intended to pre-inspect the games on the midway prior to the fair opening. This went over like a lead balloon. He was not too happy about it, so arrangements were made to visit him in the next county prior to his coming in my jurisdiction. I was to ride with an agent from our vice squad and two members of the sponsoring club. The owner of the carnival had notified the law enforcement agency in that jurisdiction about my arrival.

Once we arrived, we were met with resistance until I could convince the officers that I was not here to inspect the games, but to look around at what he offered and tell him what was not coming to our area. The two members of our local club had a meeting with him while the agent and I walked around to see what games were on the lot.

Notation was made of a few games that were not to be

brought in. After walking the midway, we met with the owner of the carnival and I had my say with him. I tried to set up a time to inspect the games when they arrived in Brunswick but could not get an answer as to what would be a good time to do this. I let him know that, if needed, we could do this while the fair was open and if we had probable cause, we would shut a game down, arrest the operator and confiscate the equipment in front of the patrons, which would put the event in a bad light.

A date and time were set. We left to return to Brunswick and I asked one of our assistant district attorneys if he could assist us on the lot that day to answer any legal questions that may arise. He agreed, and I felt better knowing we had the district attorney's office with us during this.

The group met at the designated time on the date given and we proceeded to walk around and survey what games were on the lot. Some of the games had not set up yet so we had to get the owner to contact the game owners to do that for us, so we could look at the game and answer questions about it. Getting cooperation from them was like pulling teeth.

Finally, the owner had a "Church Call" with all the game operators in front of his trailer. We intended to videotape our inspection and fill out papers that documented what we did. I had papers xeroxed that showed what was expected of the game owners and agents who worked for them and what the consequences would be for violations. I found a few of these papers laying on the ground prior to our leaving.

Our team went around with the owner to each of the games. Some games required a little modification to make it fair to both the player and game agent. A couple were shut down as they violated our laws on gambling and the games that used skilled and no gaffs could open. I allowed a couple of games to open as it proved to be a favorite with the patrons in the past.

We finished the inspection process and had a debriefing with all involved law enforcement personnel. I said that I did not trust some of the people and thought we may need to have undercover officers monitoring the players at certain games.

Before we left, the owner came toward us and made a statement that he had several other venues he serviced and did not need this shit. I did not know how serious he was until the next year when I was notified that he was not going to come back and honor the last two years on his contract. This meant we had to work with a new company.

I looked at the mistakes made from our first inspection and worked on correcting them. Although not fully pleased with the inspection, I felt good that we had done our best to keep people from getting ripped off. I often wondered if we should have stormed in during the event when it was open and hit them hard and fast. I decided that would have been a bad move and made relations with our local sponsoring club have a bad taste in their mouth about us.

I was able to acquire some crooked carnival games from a friend of mine who I met at the PACC conferences. I started instructing courses for law enforcement on this subject matter and had a good lesson plan written for a two-day course. Other carnival components I was able to attain from the carnival game owners when I inspected throughout the years. One such owner, who owned the "Knock down the Bottles" game, had three bottles weighing under three pounds but bases that were large. I asked him about those bottles and he said he was giving them to me.

After instructing a few classes on carnival game fraud, I decided to take the lesson plans and my experiences on the midway and turn it into a book for law enforcement to read. Carnival Cop was my second book written. I had pictures of certain games inspected along with the inspection details that would assist someone going in on this detail. All the papers used were shown to document what was done during this detail so if a case was made, a good report could be made showing the probable cause to make an arrest and case. And, testimony given in court would help with the prosecution.

I also instructed classes on con games at our agency as well as the police academies. I loved using the magic tricks to illustrate some of the scams as the attendee's were able to see what was being said by the effect of the trick, therefore retention of the message was kept. This was the same with the police magic routines. The children would see what was said and remember the message as it was shown via a magic trick. This is known as the "Vividness Principle".

I instructed several agencies to include, local, state and federal on bunco crime. One agent who attended an in-house class loved the style of presentation I had. He set up a class for me to instruct at the Federal Law Enforcement Training Center. I was pleased to see the reviews given by the feds on the class. I went through several scams during the day and demonstrated them. Although the only ones in the class who would do an arrest and prosecution were some local officers, the feds loved knowing the principles of the scam to prevent and protect themselves and others.

Many of the schools used my Police Magic routines during the Red Ribbon week activities. I did shows with anti-drug themes, stranger danger and obeying rules and laws. Patrolman Potbelly Pigg reinforced the messages when he appeared after the show to speak with the students about what they just witnessed. The only drawback to these shows and presentations was I did them while on duty. This meant

I could not charge a fee as I was being paid by the county at the time. This somewhat hurt my business when I was transferred back to patrol and wanted to charge a fee since I was not on duty. Many of the presentations for children were done with me wearing the police uniform to show police were your friends. For adults, I wore a business suit with a breast plate badge or a golf shirt with our badge on it.

The lesson plans I developed for the con game classes, along with the reports I had taken over the years on victims who were duped by the con artists made enough material for me to put it in a book. I wrote my third book on con games which is titled "Deceptive Performances". I liked being able to call myself an author and show the books written over the years. Sales were pretty good at first and I was able to purchase them at a discounted price to sell at my lectures and presentations.

Murder of Grand Daughter

When we had a new chief appointed, he made some changes to personnel. After I had worked as the DARE officer, Crime Prevention officer, Public Relations officer, Public Information officer, Instructor and front desk officer, I was reassigned back to patrol. I did not mind it so much as I liked the work schedule of working five days with four days off, if you did not have court those days.

In 2009, my 17-month old grand daughter was murdered by my daughter's boyfriend, who was not the biological father. I had spent some time that afternoon with her at the apartment they lived in. She enjoyed the antics with me that afternoon. I remember seeing the sadness in her face when I had to leave. I only wish I had known what was to transpire after I left.

I was visiting my former lieutenant at the hospital. He had a leg amputated and was recovering. We were best friends as I worked with him in the training division and spent many hours on special details we were assigned. We got along great. I got a phone call from my daughter, Kim, who said that she was at school in Jacksonville, Florida and got a call from her boyfriend who said that Brianna was not breathing, and they had called an ambulance. I rushed out of the hospital to their apartment only to see the ambulance coming out of the complex.

I followed it to the emergency room at the hospital and went inside with my grand daughter laying supine on the stretcher and having an ashen color on her body. I talked with her while going into the ER until a nurse took me to a private waiting room. I made notifications to my family of what was happening.

I prayed that God would look after my grand daughter and help her recover from whatever it was that she was going through. Shortly after the notifications, family members started to arrive and join me in the waiting room, which was private and away from the general population. A nurse or doctor would come in every now and then and give us a prognosis on my grand- daughter.

A little later, two of our detectives entered and I spoke with the lead investigator. He was taking my daughter's boyfriend in for questioning as was protocol in situations like this. I asked him if he suspected the boyfriend causing this? He said that may be a possibility. I then said something I should not have said, but the investigator knew my emotions were strained.

My daughter was driving from Jacksonville and I told her to stop at the state line and a county officer would pick her up. I did not want her driving while she worried about her daughter. One of our officers picked her up and brought her to the hospital. Arrangements were being made to life flight Brianna to Savannah to the children's hospital there as she could get better care.

Debbie, and Kim drove to Savannah. I had to get Kim's vehicle, so my brother drove me to the state line and I drove it to Kim's house where my other daughter's Christine and Karen rode with me to Savannah. We got to the hospital in

Savannah and found which floor we needed to go. We met Debbie after getting off the elevator and received the most horrible news. She said that Brianna was not going to make it. They had her on life support and that was the only thing keeping her alive.

After collecting myself, I notified the lead investigator about this and he made the trip to Savannah. When possible, he interviewed Kim and me about the days activities and told Kim that he suspected her boyfriend. Kim was still in a state of shock and could not believe that her boyfriend could have anything to do with this. Kim also had a decision to make that night. She had to decide if Brianna was going to be taken off life support. One of the hardest decisions she ever had to make in her life.

Brianna was taken off life support as there was no hope for her. Half her brain had flattened, and the doctor told the investigator she suspected abuse from the evidence shown on her little body. We all were in the room while Kim held Brianna as her life was slipping away. Brianna was pronounced dead about 3:30am on May 1, 2009. I went outside to smoke a cigarette and speak with the investigator. After that, I planned for a local funeral home to pick my grand daughter's body up from the crime lab when they finished the autopsy.

Karen and Christine drove their mother's car home. I drove Kim and Debbie back to Brunswick. On arrival at Kim's house, she left to go to the apartment against my wishes. I stayed at her house with Debbie and finally got the chance to cry. I had to stay strong for them earlier, but I let it out then.

The investigation continued into the death of my grand daughter and the chief called me on the phone. We spoke for a short time as I was in no condition to talk. Other friends contacted me after hearing the news as well. I was not up to speaking with anyone at that time. We tried to get Kim to come back to her house to stay with family, but she insisted on staying at the apartment where she and Bri had lived for a short time.

When my grand daughter's body was released, we had to make funeral arrangements. Kim, Debbie, Karen, Christine and I went to the funeral home to make the arrangements. I hated seeing my daughter going through the same thing I had to do when my son was killed. The emotions welled up in me.

I did not like Kim living at the apartment while she was going through this. Family members from New York traveled down to Brunswick for the funeral. She needed to be with family. The funeral home staff were so good to me and my family during all this. They helped us get through this tragedy.

I planned to have Kim speak to a local psychologist after she tried to hurt herself. During her interview with the doctor, the lead investigator called me saying that that her boyfriend was being charged with Felony Murder and Cruelty to Children 1st, both felonies. I waited until Kim had finished her session with the doctor to tell her. I spoke to the doctor in private first before telling Kim.

I was told the son of my daughter's boyfriend had witnessed his father slamming my grand-daughter's head on the floor that day. He was interviewed by the investigator and gave testimony that was consistent with the evidence shown on her body. I never understood what that man had against my grand-daughter as she was such a sweet little girl.

Being that the accused murderer was incarcerated, he would not be attending the funeral. We had Bri dressed in the outfit she was baptized in. It was a white gown with a white bonnet. Looking at her in the casket seemed as if she was asleep but I knew she would not awaken. I gave her a kiss on the head and told her that I wished I had known so I could have saved her from that monster.

The viewing was attended by many people that night. A good portion of those in attendance were law enforcement from the area agencies. My daughter, Karen, put together a video to play with music for people to see pictures of Bri and her family. I remember standing there watching those memories and crying like a baby. My former sister in law, Carol, came over and put her hand on my shoulder in support while I watched the video.

The next day was the service and funeral. The minister who baptized Bri spoke followed by me, my daughters, Karen and Kim. The procession to the gravesite was escorted by members of the Glynn County Police and I thanked the officers who stood at attention at intersections as we passed by. We arrived at the gravesite where my grandson, Jaime, my son in law, Kevin, myself and two others carried the casket to the final resting place.

The minister made some remarks and the service ended. Our family went to my brother's house where the reception was held. I went to PAMS Law Enforcement Dinner Club to pick up the food Pam Hammer had prepared for us. We spent time at my brother's house eating, talking about Bri and mingling with others there. My son in law, Kevin, and I acted the fool when music was playing. It was a way to break the somber mood we all felt.

The trial for the accused murderer of my grand-daughter was coming up. I had spoken with the district attorney's office and was to testify. I did not want my daughter, Kim, testifying as she would have to look at pictures of the autopsy and I did not want her to have to go through that. I waited upstairs until I was called.

The doctor who was at the children's hospital in Savannah had already testified as had the paramedic who was on the call. I testified and had to be shown the pictures of the autopsy which tore my heart apart. I also identified Brianna's shirt and told about my visit there that day. We broke for lunch and I had to resume testimony on the stand after lunch.

Others gave testimony to include the doctor who did the autopsy of Brianna. Diagrams, pictures and oral testimony were shown on the autopsy. The son of the accused testified against his father. The defense attempted to discredit him, but he did an excellent job giving his statement on what he witnessed that day. I was so proud of him. He was only 8 years old when he witnessed this tragedy.

The accused was charged with Malice Murder, Felony Murder and Cruelty to Children 1st. I did not understand why the Grand Jury included Malice Murder as I felt the accused did not intend to kill Brianna, only injure her. Felony Murder in Georgia is where a person, in the commission of another felony (Cruelty to Children 1st) kills another person. I did not see how he would be found guilty of Malice Murder.

The jury went out to deliberate. When we were called back in, we listened to the foreman of the jury say they acquitted the accused of Malice Murder, which I knew they would, but they hung on the other two charges, which I could not understand as the burden of proof had been shown. I was upset and angry with the verdict. Afterward, we met with the District Attorney to see about getting a new trial on the remaining charges.

Debbie was livid as was the rest of the family. Prior to this trial, the jail had the bail reduced so the accused could be released as his kidney dialysis treatments were cutting into their budget. Debbie went on a media rampage against this which caused us to be brought into the district attorney's office. I understood why the decision was made as I worked for the county and knew about the budgets.

Before leaving that meeting, I assured the district attorney that I would move into Kim's house and stay with them to help them feel safe as the accused was going to stay at his grandmother's house not too far down the street. Although Debbie and I had divorced years earlier, we remained good friends. I took up with Maria shortly after the divorce and moved into her house. I hated leaving my girlfriend's house, but Maria understood the concern and supported this move for now.

A new trial date was set for August of 2012, just a year and a half after the first trial. An assistant district attorney, who assisted with the first trial, was the lead prosecutor this time. She did a fantastic job proving the accused was responsible for my grand-daughter's death. Again, I testified on the events of the day when I was there. The same doctors from the first trial testified again, as did the son of the accused.

After about three days, the prosecutor and defense made their closing arguments to the triers of fact. We left the courtroom to await the jury's verdict. I had hoped and prayed that this jury would see the evidence and render a guilty verdict this time around. We were summoned back into court a few hours later for the verdict.

The verdict was read. Guilty on Felony Murder and Cruelty to Children 1st. The judge imposed the sentence on the convicted man. Life imprisonment. Nowadays, a life sentence meant you had to serve 30 years before eligible for parole. When the woman who killed my son was given a life sentence back in 1977, you only had to serve 7 years, so

I was glad the law had changed. The convicted man hung his head in disbelief and was escorted out of the courtroom by sheriffs' deputies. I was so happy that this had now come to an end but knew appeals would be part of the process.

The convicted man served five years in prison before passing away. I felt no remorse for him but did feel bad for his children as I knew they loved him. Now, both people who murdered family members were dead and neither one ever showed remorse or apologized for taking their lives. Closure had not come to me in my son's murder nor had it come to me with the murder of my grand-daughter. I told my family that closure will come with my last breath.

Police Magic

To better understand what Police Magic is, I tell people it is using magic and puppets for crime/drug/bunco prevention presentations.

Magic tricks are routined to show certain themes while the bunco shows will also use magic to illustrate certain points, equipment such as carnival games will allow the audience to witness how laws of physics, principles of magic and science are used to deceive the people.

As mentioned earlier, routines on anti-drug messages, personal safety, traffic, gun safety, peer pressure, good citizenship, obeying rules and laws, vandalism to property, being jailed, self-esteem, stranger danger and other topics are used for the youth.

For the adults, topics include home security, personal safety, con games and carnival game fraud issues. I did a host of Neighborhood Watch presentations where I demonstrated these routines. The adults loved watching and being entertained while learning crime prevention tips to help them be safe. This was a highlight of my job when I worked those 11 years in administration.

Over the years, the many presentations presented along with the training classes for law enforcement personnel showed me that there was significant interest in these. I have been approached by many who remarked how much they loved the presentations or classes and many who said they remember me doing these years ago.

I also used puppets to reinforce the messages or used them solo to talk about the messages conveyed. It was not only fun, but enjoyable for everyone involved. I still look for magic tricks that I can routine into new messages or update the old ones that were used. My former son in law remarked how he remembered when I brought the pig puppet to his class when he was in elementary school and that sparked his interest in becoming a law enforcement officer.

The next chapter will show the puppets I have used and the purpose for each one.

Puppets

As mentioned in an earlier chapter, I showed where I started out with the McGruff puppet our agency had in storage. It was to be used with taped programs for children, but no one was doing that. I could keep the puppet with me and I practiced with it for many days and nights to see if I could speak about the programs McGruff is known for.

I was still a novice to ventriloquism but with the help of Cliff Patton and observing his puppet shows, I was able to work out a style of presentation that was comfortable to me. McGruff reinforced the Police Magic shows presented and spoke to the youth on a variety of issues they needed to hear. I liked this better than having to don the costume we had. It was too hot and humid here in the South to be wearing that costume outside.

Over time, I wanted to get another puppet that would be closer to our agency with the same uniform. I came up with getting a pig puppet. People asked why a pig puppet? First, children seemed to be more receptive to animal puppets and second, police were called "PIGS" by certain groups. However, PIG became an acronym and we made it stand for Pride, Integrity and Guts. I was able to obtain a small uniform shirt along with a small pair of pants that was altered to fit the size of the pig puppet.

Once the puppet was designed, the clothes were altered to fit it. I sent a couple of shoulder patches to the designer and he had them sewn on the shirt sleeves. Then, he went out and got some children toys with a police theme. A plastic Glock type gun, a whistle, handcuffs, baton and radio. He had a belt made that had a gun holster, handcuff holster, radio holster as well as a regular belt under this to secure with velcro loops.

Finally, he made a few campaign police type hats and sent a pair of cool looking sunglasses too. When the puppet arrived, I decorated the shirt with other things to include a badge, name plate and collar brass. I put a pin of McGruff on it as well since this was the first puppet I started out with. The name given this puppet was Patrolman Potbelly Pigg and he even had an official police ID made. I used the school safety patrol badge for his campaign hat as it was small enough to place on it.

The pig puppet and the McGruff puppet sometimes would interact together with me. This proved somewhat difficult as I kept forgetting which voice to use and would have McGruff sounding like the pig puppet and vice versa. This did work out good though as I used it as a comedy routine where they stole each other's voice and it became a great part of the routine. The bad part was both of my hands and arms were used to manipulate the puppets, so I could not use them for anything else.

Pre-K, Kindergarten and First grades loved the puppets and the antics of each one. We mostly spoke on stranger danger issues and safety at school and home. When word got around about this, it seemed like a domino effect as I got calls to perform at many daycares and other children after school programs. Although I was pleased with the responses, it did take a toll on me after a while. I was known as the puppet policeman as the moniker was given by staff members.

When I no longer did presentations for the department and was reassigned back to patrol, I changed the persona of the pig puppet. I took the shoulder patches off, and anything else that showed it as a member of our agency. I then put a sheriff's star on the shirt and hat, boots to replace the shoes and renamed it Sheriff Buford P. Swine.

I wondered how adults would react to a puppet. I thought about a puppet that could do magic for my regular magic shows and speak on bunco. Speaking to the puppet designer who had made the pig puppet, he suggested a human looking puppet dressed in a tux. He asked what type of face I wanted, and I said with blue eyes, as my girlfriend, Maria, loved my blue eyes and sport a mustache and goatee. Hair color would be salt and pepper as my hair was graying at the time.

The puppet designer sent me the puppet when finished and I loved his look. I put a chain over the vest to dress it up a bit and picked out a hat for it to wear. I wondered about his name and the voice I would use. Combining my last name and Houdini's name, it was called Hesteni. The voice would be an older gruffer type voice like that of a dirty old man.

I used Hesteni for my adult magic shows and had it speak on con games when I demonstrated some con game themes with magic. Hesteni is limited in what it can do with magic, but I found a few tricks that it could do with me using only one hand. One routine I love is James Munton's "Little Book of Quotes", a mind reading routine. It is easy to do as I will have Hesteni divine the one word in a quote the volunteer selects.

Nowadays, he is used for just regular magic shows as I have other crime prevention puppets for those routines.

After Hesteni came the Inspector. The local civic club, the Jay Cee's, wanted to help so they purchased the Inspector for me after I did a presentation for their group. At first, I called it Inspector Jay Cee but have since changed its name to Inspector F. A. Raud (Fraud) since it speaks on bunco themes like con games and carnival game fraud. The voice I chose for the inspector is more a Columbo and Dirty Harry combined.

A friend of mine, Brian Douglas, who is stationed overseas, is an artist who has used my puppets in strips of comics for humor and educational aspects. He has been working on a comic series that teaches children certain lessons from the stranger danger program. Hesteni, the Inspector and Sheriff Buford are featured in this media. I hope to have this book sometime soon to distribute to children as it is a great avenue for them to learn about safety issues for themselves.

My last puppet is an idea I had after Brian made a strip on me after I had my open-heart surgery. He showed me recovering with the scar down my chest and said I was barely alive. The premise was to make me the first police magician puppet man. Then, he showed my three puppets working on me like that of the 6-million-dollar man theme. The outcome was a drawing of me like a puppet man dressed in my police uniform.

I found a puppet maker who created look alike puppets. I contacted him about making me one and sent him pictures of my facial features. I wanted him to put the puppet in a gray shirt and black pants. I already had a badge made with my name on it and the police magic wording as well as a name plate I had when I was in military school in 1965.

When the puppet arrived, I adorned it with these items as well as a police magic wristband and other items to personalize it. I also placed one of my police magician ball caps on the head. I placed them in a cabinet that now holds the Police Magician puppet, Sheriff Buford and the Inspector. I had to purchase another cabinet to hold Hesteni as there was not room for a fourth puppet. I tell people that Hesteni was put in a separate cabinet as he tried to corrupt the crime prevention puppets.

I use this puppet for everything the other two crime prevention puppets can do. One thing I told my grandchildren about this puppet was that when I die, my soul will go into it and it will become me. Their eyes got big after hearing that. Of course, my daughters made me tell them the truth that it won't come alive after I die. The voice I use on the Police Magician puppet is a high shrill type voice like Jeff Dunham's "Little Jeff" puppet.

How do I transport each of the puppets? Glad you asked. For Sheriff Buford, I have a bag with the patch on the outside showing "SHERIFF". In the bag are items like a set of handcuffs using hands instead of the rachet on it. Hesteni has his own suitcase table that was made by Showtime Magic that he will fit in for shows. The Inspector has a large footlocker looking case decorated with bunco themes and the police magic emblem. The Police Magician puppet has a bag with a "Police" patch on the outside.

I always try to bring a puppet with me to any event where Police Magic will be shown. Sheriff Buford primarily will be used for Stranger Danger for the children nowadays and talk about anti-drug messages and personal safety for other events. The Inspector will speak with adults on bunco themes when needed and Hesteni will go with me to magic shows to entertain with some magic and comedy of his own. If the audience is made up of mixed ages the Police Magician puppet will be brought in to speak on a variety of issues.

My daughter, Christine, who spent 13 years in law enforcement, used to assist me in magic shows when she was younger. I had hoped she would be interested in taking this over one day, but she no longer works law enforcement and is raising two of my grandchildren. Besides, she said she is not interested in puppets.

Con Games

One thing I do when instructing classes on con games, either to law enforcement or the public, is to survey audience members on what they know about it, have they been conned and what type of reports were taken from victims. I also ask if they have attempted to con others and give a description of how it was done.

One student in law enforcement gave a great response. He said that he told a woman, "Of course I will respect you in the morning" when asked how he would feel after having sex with her. Others mentioned how they called into work feigning sickness when they were healthy or lying to their wives to save face when asked if they performed a chore she asked him to do.

One of the saddest information shown was the mindset of some law enforcement officers on how they felt about some of the victims after taking their report. Some have stated that the victim deserved what they got for being greedy. I do not cotton to this mindset and have spoken out against it. I let the attendees know that the scenarios of many of these con games are played out so well that the victim felt they were in control and had a stake in the outcome.

To get them to feel somewhat like a victim, I do certain things to show how easy it is for even them to be conned.

Some of the magic tricks I do or using actual components of a con game, like the Hanky Switch, assist in this segment. Misdirection, sleight of hand, two principles of magic are used in the Hanky Switch to deceive the victim. I switch the handkerchief with the real money in it to one that has cut up paper to resemble the shape of the money. Their faces are priceless when they open the switched handkerchief.

Magic tricks like the 3 ½ of Clubs is used to show how con games make the impossible possible. The way this trick works is for the volunteer to either choose a card from another deck (which will be the seven of clubs) or take a pair of dice and choose one of them. The volunteer will turn away from me and look at the top number. Whichever number chosen, they will look on the bottom and add those two numbers together, which will be a 7. I then go through a routine to get them to choose, without them knowing it, a suit of clubs. Then, I have them divide that number by two. They say it cannot be done most times. I tell them to divide it by two and give me the answer. They say 3.5 or three and a half. I then refer them to the suit they chose, clubs, and say you want me to come up with a 3 ½ of Clubs? I then tell them that they want me to make the impossible possible and pick up the large card on the table which shows the 3 ½ of Clubs.

Martin Lewis has a four-card trick named Sidewalk Shuffle that shows that nothing is as it seems in a con game. I show one large card that is an Ace of Clubs, and three large blank cards. The premise is to follow the cards when shuffled. Unless I want them to win, I will show they were wrong in their choice. At the end, I mention that one card was shown to be printed, the Ace of Clubs. The other three were blank. Then, I tell them that nothing is at it seems when involved in a con game and show only one blank card and three Ace of Clubs.

These tricks allow the attendees to see how it feels to be duped and further have more empathy for victims. I also feel that they will be able to write a better report knowing how the con is worked and the elements of the crime. Seeing how some of the games are played and the secret to each one will assist them in court should they have to demonstrate this for the judge and triers of fact. It is most important to know how these are done if you are prosecuting a case.

I remember one such case our department was involved with years ago. A person came in to make a report on the loss of company money. The victim told the officer that he was robbed of the money. The way he explained how he was robbed did not meet the elements of the crime. He mentioned a card game, which was a clue, as the FBI would say, that this was more of a 3 Card Monte scam. This was done at one of our rest-stops. Officers went out to the area and arrested four men who were scamming people with this.

They were brought into the station and I started speaking with them. Pretending not to have knowledge of how the game was played, one of the men, the tosser, demonstrated for me and a couple of other officers. Thinking I would not find the money card, the tosser was surprised when I found it each time. I wanted to fuck with him a few more times but one of the officers stated that I was a magician and taught this to other officers. Yes, I knew the sleight of hand technique used and could follow the money card each time as he did not deviate from the routine.

Using magic as well as showing the components of certain street scams assisted my training classes to educate law enforcement. I had some of the attendees work on the mechanics of each scam to see if they could perform it in court to show how the crime was committed. Some were able to do this after a little practice while others needed to practice it much more before they became proficient with it.

When asked if I was ever conned, I reply about the change raising scam I encountered while a teenager working in a news and record shop. I got clipped for 40 dollars that night. I also say I have been married three times as well so that should count as a con too.

Another aspect of Police Magic in the Fraud aspect would be inspection of crooked carnival games and those games where gambling laws were violated.

Carnival Game Fraud

I never thought I would ever learn the secrets to the ways I was ripped off at the games on the midways of the many carnivals and fairs attended over the years, but that changed after I got into law enforcement. As mentioned earlier, I met an investigator in another state who was well versed in con games and carnival game fraud.

Bruce Walstad gave seminars on these subjects. I requested attending one of his week-long seminars in Florida and my chief granted me the time to go to school. Bruce did segments on con games and when finished, started on the crooked carnival games. He had the classroom looking like a mini-midway. Games that could be played honest and crooked, games that gave the player no chance of winning as well as games that violated gambling laws as well as a host of others were shown, demonstrated and explained. I felt like I was in Heaven.

Now, I could see how I was ripped off all these years and do something about it. I had to remember to be a professional and not let feelings of revenge overtake me. In later years, I felt I could get even with the crooked carnival personnel by implementing regulations in our state that would stop them from bringing in games that ripped people off. I have gone through this process two times with different legislators of our state and am currently working on this a third time with a legislator that I am friends with.

I don't know if our state will implement any regulations, but I must give it the old college try. One thing that tells me this may not happen is what a carnival owner told me years ago. He was the first carnival I inspected and later inspected on a military base after giving the CID unit and military police a two-day seminar on the crooked games. This owner said that I would never get regulations in our state as the carnival industry has the politicians in their pockets. Considering the hit and miss with the other two attempts with the legislators, I felt he may have been correct.

I was fortunate to be able to acquire some of the crooked games through a friend of mine with the state fair police in my early years. I then got others from the owners and agents who gave me the components of their game. I was honest with them and told them I wanted to use it in training classes, so I was surprised they gave it up.

I have used these games in training classes for law enforcement as well as show them to the public at special events. One such event was at our local mall that had the area packed with adults and children. I had my friend from the Brunswick Police Department, Bob May, who was also a magician and had taken over the inspection of the local fair. Sadly, the video I have of this does not have audio, but when shown, I explain the game to the class and what is about to transpire.

One group who has had me three times was the state science educators of Georgia. Twice I did presentations for about an hour and a half each on Jekyll Island, Georgia and once at a college in mid Georgia where they had me for three hours. Laws of physics, principles of magic and science were shown as well as the laws of probability to the attendees.

They were able to play the games and see which principles were used to deceive the player. I explained what "Flat, Two Way, Chance (gambling), Skill, Percentage, Group, Hanky Pank and Alibi Games" were. If you want to know this as well, please purchase my Carnival Cop book.

I have been told that many people have expressed appreciation for this type training to keep them safe from the crooked carnival personnel. Please don't get me wrong. I do not think that all carnival personnel are crooked. There are many decent and hard-working people who travel to different venues to work their trade for a living. The ones I am concerned about are those who ply their trade to rip people off from hard- earned money. I have always stated that any game which gives the player little or no chance of winning is no longer a game. It is a crime of Theft by Deception per Georgia standards and known by other statues in other states.

Finding magic routines that would fit certain themes on this subject matter was a little difficult, but I was able to find a few. Showing the game, demonstrating it and allowing others to play it to see which principle used was easy. How could I demonstrate, with magic, about some of these? I found four which could show certain things with it. One trick that I use to show how the player wins a small prize and must trade up by continuing the play uses four lollipops in a paper sack. I show each one and take one, that is my favorite, and place it in my pocket. I ask what type of prize you may win at a game and have the volunteer reach into the bag to pull the contents out. They pull out fake poop, which I say may be a prize that is nothing more than crap.

For the attraction of the "Guess your Weight/Age" I use a magician's utility prop that is used for mind reading. Since I don't want to reveal the secret here, I will just say that I can write the answer down on a piece of paper that will match whatever the volunteer tells me after I make my choice. This is shown in my Police Magician book under the carnival section. There are two other tricks I use to show that all those expensive prizes like televisions, stereo players or camcorders will never leave the shelves with you or how some games give you little or no chance of winning, to include the gambling games.

This is one of my favorite areas of instructing as I am still a kid at heart and love presenting this to people, whether law enforcement or members of the general- public. I often wonder who will get all my magic and carnival games when I pass away. I hope whoever gets them will use them and benefit from it. Except that I do not want anyone using the crooked carnival games to profit. I remember how some groups have requested the games for their benefits, but I could not allow it as the games are crooked, not honest.

Retirement

After five years with the Sullivan County Sheriffs Office in upstate New York plus 25 years with Glynn County police, I thought 30 years was long enough for me in law enforcement. About a year prior to my retirement, I spoke with Human Resources on what I needed to do to collect my pension. I was given an outline for money, after taxes and insurance, that I would receive. I thought, not bad, but knew I would need another job to help sustain me as I had debts owed and needing to pay monthly.

Years ago, when we had the G8 Summit in our area, I had spoken with retired officers who were working for the United States Secret Service as Special Officers. They would go through training and be armed, working different venues around the world on protective detail for the POTUS and staff as well as other dignitaries that were assigned to that division.

I looked up the job on the internet but was saddened to find that the job was no longer used for retired officers as they had an age cut off on it. You could not be over 37 years old now. Well, my dreams for this job went out the window. I wondered if I could do magic and the police magic shows to help sustain an income. I contacted a booking agency and promoted my website on other areas to get my name out there. The problem with our area was many did not like the price charged for a 45-minute presentation or show and I did not like having to travel long distances to do a show and then drive back.

When the time came for my last day at work, I used it to bring my equipment back to the station to get checked off. My lieutenant went over the vehicle and items that were in it, the quartermaster went over the uniforms and gear that I had to turn in. The last part was a sad one for me as it would be the last time I spoke on the radio. I called dispatch and went 10-42, which is ending tour of duty and 10-7 which is out of service. I also said how much I enjoyed working with all the staff during these 25 years and listened as several people wished me farewell and best of luck in my retirement.

The county gave me nine extra months for service due to the sick time I accrued over the months and paid me for over four hundred hours of vacation time. Part of this money was used for my retirement party at PAMS Law Enforcement Dinner Club. I had my grandsons wedding reception there a few years earlier and witnessed what a great catering event this was and wanted Pam and Bob Hammer to host my retirement as well.

The night of the party, the place was jammed packed with invitees with most of them being law enforcement and many friends along with family members. I was enjoying the night when I got a surprise. One of my former high school classmates arrived and said a few words on my behalf. My former shift, who had taken me out prior to my retirement to dinner and the Comedy Club, had a plaque given to me with each of their names on it. Also, a book with many officers and staff writing their well wishes in it with some comedy statements about me was presented. My chief gave me a plaque with an inscription of my years of service with the agency and a clock was on it. The chief also gave me a retirement badge with the Glock firearm, which was placed in a shadow box, that I had used when active.

My magician/ventriloquist friend, Cliff Patton, came down to do a show for the adults and children there as well as singing a song about my retirement that he composed. I was astonished with many of the gifts given me. My daughters made me items about my retirement that I hold dear to my heart today and have them hanging on the wall in my room. Pam Hammer had a beautiful glass mug made with our patch and my name, badge number and years of service with GCPD. Also given were many gift certificates to dine at PAMS. I would never be hungry again with all of this.

It was a great evening, and all had a good time. The food, fellowship and activities proved to be a show of love for me. I made an announcement that I knew the cops were only here for the free food and drinks, but I was not paying for their alcohol. This got some laughter as I was saying this in jest, but serious about not paying for the booze. Pam and her staff did a fantastic job. I had dined there over the years as well as have her cater many events for me during these years, so I had no doubt she would have put on a good spread for those in attendance at the retirement party.

The next day reality set in as I had to make plans to seek employment to supplement my pension before the money received from the county ran out. I made application at many places, even applying to do housekeeping at a local resort hotel as I was not proud. Then, a ray of hope came up. A couple of retired officers from the city police were working at the federal building next to the post office. I stopped in and spoke with them on this type of job. They were employed with a security agency who was assigned to the United States Marshals Service as Court Security Officers. Having worked protective details in the past, I thought this would be good for me. They gave me the info needed to get the ball rolling.

I made application but did not hear anything for awhile as there was no openings available at that time. I kept checking to see if the job listing came up, but each day checked made my heart sink as nothing was showing. I applied to work with a local resort just down the road from where I lived. I had worked part time with them in the past when I was an active law enforcement officer. My former chief was the director of security there and hired me. I worked a few days a week as they were grooming me for a couple of special details. I worked many different assignments given until I got somewhat discouraged with it and resigned.

I was unemployed for awhile until I got a call from the manager of the agency who hired people to work as a federal court security officer. I went to Savannah for an interview and filled out more paperwork. Now it was a waiting game. A few months later, I got a call about an opening and was asked if I accepted the position. I said I would and was told to come back to Savannah to be fingerprinted and fill out more paperwork. From time of application to starting work was about nine months. An extensive background check was part of it from Homeland Security. I had a few more meetings with Homeland Security and the manager before I was given a start date.

Finally, I started at the federal building and was glad to be working among people I knew. They were great showing me the ropes and helping me get decked out in the uniform. I had to get pants, shoes, shirts, tie and blazers that were part of the uniform. I filled out more paperwork with the manager and was awaiting an opening to attend the US Marshals Academy at the Federal Law Enforcement Center, aka Homeland Security.

My first day I had to qualify with their weapon on the range. I observed the other officers in their roles, studied the standard operating procedures for my job and learned about our protective detail. We were responsible for another federal court in another county. It was a much smaller building, but I enjoyed going there and working with another officer. I got to work the x-ray machine and magnetometer when people would arrive. I had a sense of purpose now and loved the responsibilities and duties.

About seven months after being hired and several times bumped from attending the Marshal's academy, I finally got in a class. At that time, it was only a three-day class where nowadays they do a full week. I was still able to do magic shows and police magic presentations at night or weekends as this job worked during the day and hardly ever had you stay over late, unless one of the judges was still in the building. Although listed as part time, I worked forty hours each week as we were shorthanded. When finished with the Marshal's academy, I was given an FTO to evaluate me before letting me work solo. Once cleared, I loved not having to be with another officer as I liked working without supervision.

About ten months into this job, I was diagnosed with blockage in my neck and legs by Dr. Jennifer Miller. I had to undergo some testing and get cleared to return to work as the Marshals had strict standards. I underwent a test to show that the blockage was 99% on the left side of my neck and the pain I felt in my legs showed blockage as well. I returned to work until I was told I had to undergo surgery on the left side of my neck. July 2, 2015 was the date set for me to go to Jacksonville, Florida to get it repaired. I was to be off about a week after that and return to work until the Marshals had me undergo a stress test. The local cardiologist, Dr. Matthew Certain, who was a former student of mine in the

DARE program years ago, said I needed to have a heart cath asap.

The cath showed I had blockage on my heart as well. Two sides showed 90% blockage and the back side showed 100% blockage. The doctor told me, my girlfriend, Maria and my daughter, Kim that I would need open heart surgery. I notified my boss at work, so they knew I would not be back to work for a while. The next month I underwent open heart surgery and recovered at home. My daughter, Karen, came down to assist Maria with my recovery. Karen brought my grandson, Tyrus, and he assisted with my exercises.

I was informed that the next month I was scheduled to have the operation on my right leg which would require at least 8 weeks recovery. I notified my boss at work on this as well. I was beginning to feel that I would never get back to work. The bad thing was, no work, no money. The only money coming in was my pension, which was not good enough to make my debts each month. After my right leg surgery, I recovered at home with Karen still there to look after me. My cardiologist planned for me to go to cardiac rehab at our local hospital. When I was well enough to travel, I made an appointment to fill out paperwork and see about a start date.

The surgeon in Jacksonville wanted to do my left leg but I told him I needed a break as I had three surgeries back to back and could not start rehab if I had to recover another 8 weeks again. I held off until April of the next year to get the left leg done. Then, in November I had the right side of the neck done. This was five surgeries. Finances were not that good after the first three surgeries, so my daughter applied on my behalf for Social Security Disability. I would be 62 in January of 2016, the next year, so I could apply for retirement then.

However, Karen notified each of my creditors about my surgeries and told them I only had my pension coming in. They worked with me as long as they could, but time was approaching for me to make some payments. I kept up the bills I could on the necessary debts. I sought an attorney to help me file bankruptcy although I was not wanting to do this, but circumstances dictated I had no other choice. My attorney filed on my behalf at the federal building where I had worked as a court security officer. It was embarrassing to show up for that court but glad I got the unsecured debts taken care of. I was able to keep my vehicle thankfully.

I got word that my disability claim with Social Security was denied. My attorney, Richard Taylor, who did the bankruptcy, also helped me with the disability claim. I reapplied and some months later was denied once again. Finally, after two and a half years from first applying, we were able to go before an Ad Min Law Judge with Social Security and I was granted full disability as I could not return to work as a Court Security Officer doing protective detail. It took a while for them to send me the back-pay money owed but when it came in, I was so happy to see my savings account in better shape.

I went through cardiac rehab two times and once for pulmonary. I am required to sleep with a cpap machine at night as my sleep study showed me stopping breathing too many times during my sleep and for long periods of times. I also have had to lose weight or risk losing a leg or become a candidate for open heart surgery once again. I am on several medications that must be taken daily in the morning and evenings. I can no longer blow up balloons to make balloon animals at my magic shows due to COPD.

Since I am now disabled and cannot work, the only thing I can do is magic and police magic presentations. I attempted to see if the police academies could use my special programs on Police Magic and Bunco, but their budget allows only those classes that are required by Georgia POST. I have kept up with both magic and police magic by doing some presentations, but they are few and far between at this time. I had to turn down some offers as I cannot travel that far or have the strength to do them. I found out after a 45-minute presentation that it takes more out of me than expected. I tire easily with the loading, unloading, the presentation and loading and unloading after that.

Conclusion

I look back on my life and wonder if I blazed a trail that made a difference with people I encountered doing the Police Magic and puppets. I am proud of what I have achieved with the routines and messages shown to people over the years as I have seemed to overcome the learning disability I have had for so many years.

I sometimes wonder if the voice I heard that night on the beach back in July of 1977 was real and if my life with the Police Magic, puppets and regular magic was what it meant. I know that the years I taught the DARE program had many children learning about issues important to them. Those witnessing the Police Magic and police puppets learned something to help them live better lives.

My girlfriend, Maria, told me that she was impressed by my determination not to let my disability prevent my ability to inspire others. So, have I inspired others, and do I continue to do so? That will be known to those who are affected by it. It is so nice to have people come up to me and tell me they remember my being a part of their life in earlier years and how much they loved the programs I showed them.

I remember one young lady who was in a DARE class in my early years. She was a flirt with the boys and I worried that she would grow up to be loose. Years later, I met her, her husband and children. She told me how my example and presentations helped her change for the better. I was so pleased that she did not grow up like I thought she could have.

On a sad note, one child who I had contact with in the early years followed in her mother's profession of being a prostitute as well as a drug addict. I met her at our station and almost did not recognize her as the drugs changed her looks. She remembered me and told me how she enjoyed watching me do the school assemblies with the police magic and pig puppet. I asked her why she chose this profession. She said it was the only life she knew. About a year later, she was found murdered in a local city park. The investigation into her murder continues today.

The tragedy of losing my son and the despair I had that almost caused me to end my life along with the tragedy of losing my grand-daughter will forever be etched in my memory. But I look back on my life and think that the path I chose may have been the special thing the voice meant that night. And that may be the Triumph achieved. This was my path to Police Magic.